ENTRY LEVEL CERTIFICATE

Information and Communication Technology

Alun Hinder

JOHN MURRAY

Entry Level Certificate books:
Entry Level Certificate Information and Communication Technology ISBN 0 7195 7185 5
Entry Level Certificate Information and Communication Technology Teacher's Resource Book ISBN 0 7195 7186 3

Certificate of Achievement books:
Certificate of Achievement French ISBN 0 7195 7622 9
Certificate of Achievement French Teacher's Resource Book ISBN 0 7195 7623 7
Certificate Science for NEAB Biology ISBN 0 7195 7515 X
Certificate Science for NEAB Chemistry ISBN 0 7195 7514 1
Certificate Science for NEAB Physics ISBN 0 7195 7513 3
Certificate Science for NEAB Teacher's Resource File ISBN 0 7195 7516 8

Acknowledgements
The publishers are grateful to the following for permission to reproduce copyright photographs:

Ros Chapman (p.5), Andrew Brookes/Corbis (cover), John Townson/CREATION (pp2 *left*, 10 *both*, 11 *top*, 20, 56 *top*, 57 *both*), Economatics (Education) Ltd (p.50), hightechphotos.com (p.13 *bottom*), Tom Way/IBM Corporation (p.4 *top*), Last Resort Picture Library (pp3, 4 *bottom right*, 6 *both*, 7 *both*, 8 *both*, 12, 21, 26, 35, 38, 56 *bottom*), LEGO Dacta (UK) (p.55), Coolpix 885/Nikon UK (p.13 *top*), P + G Computer Products (p.11 *bottom*), Swallow Systems, High Wycombe, Bucks (p.49 *bottom*), Valiant Technology (pp9, 49 *top*)

and to the following for permission to use clip art:
Bitfolio (pp18, 22 *all*), IMSI (pp2 *right*, 4 *bottom left*)

The publishers have made every effort to trace copyright holders, but if they have inadvertently overlooked any they will be pleased to make the necessary arrangements at the earliest opportunity.

First published as *Certificate of Achievement Information Technology*
in 1999
by John Murray (Publishers) Ltd
50 Albemarle Street
London W1S 4BD

This edition first published 2002

Layouts by Wearset Ltd
Artwork by Art Construction
Cover design by John Townson/Creation
Typeset in 12/14pt Rockwell by Wearset Ltd, Boldon, Tyne and Wear
Printed and bound in Spain by Bookprint S.L., Barcelona

A catalogue entry for this title is available from the British Library.

ISBN 0 7195 7185 5
Teacher's Resource Book ISBN 0 7195 7186 3

Contents

Information Technology   2

Communicating   14

Handling Data   24

Modelling   37

Control   48

Glossary   59

Index   62

The Teacher's Resource Book

This book is accompanied by **Entry Level Certificate Information and Communication Technology** *Teacher's Resource Book*, which provides guidance for teachers, photocopiable coursework tasks for the students and detailed mark schemes, for each of the four strands: *Communicating*, *Handling Data*, *Modelling* and *Control*. Completion of the tasks successfully will allow students to attain the Entry Level Certificate.

Source of sample data for students' exercises

In the *Handling Data* and *Modelling* sections of this book and the *Teacher's Resource Book*, students work on databases and spreadsheets. The databases and spreadsheets used are available from the following web site:

http://www.advunit.demon.co.uk/ELC

The data can be downloaded in a variety of formats to suit different software.

Information Technology

What is information technology?

'The cat sat on the mat.'

The sentence above tells us something about the cat. It gives us information about the cat. We could store this information using a **computer**, along with lots of other data. Using computers to store and sort out information is called **information technology**.

Information technology is often known as IT. Nowadays the term information technology has been replaced by the term information and communication technology (ICT).

A computer is a device that is used to store data. The computer user can then retrieve data from the computer and do something useful with it.

Personal computers can be 'desktop' or 'laptop'.

The main elements of a computer are:

- the central processing unit (CPU), which does most of the work
- a keyboard to type data into the processor (input)
- a screen, or monitor, to see what you are doing and to display your results (output)
- a disk drive to store your data (storage)

You can use a computer to store all kinds of information, and then do useful things with it.

There are extra devices that you can use with a computer, such as a printer. These are called **peripherals**.

How does a computer work?

A computer is a complex electronic device. In this book, we shall not be looking at how a computer actually works, but at what we can use computers to do. In general terms, the human user asks the computer to do something, the computer works out what to do and then does it.

The parts of the computer that you can see and touch are known as the **hardware**. For example, the keyboard and monitor are hardware. The programs that control the computer are known as **software**.

Computer programs

Computer programs control what you see on the screen. A program is a set of instructions that the computer can understand. For example, a word processor is a program for entering text from a keyboard and producing documents that can be sent to a **printer**. This book was written using a word processor.

Programs are sometimes called **applications** or **packages**. The programs are loaded into the computer's **main memory** from storage devices. Once in the main memory of the computer they operate at very high speeds.

Storage

Data can be stored on a number of devices, such as hard disks, floppy disks and **CD-ROMs**. The amount of data that can be stored on a device is called its capacity. Capacity is measured in **kilobytes** (KB for short), **megabytes** (MB for short) or **gigabytes** (GB for short).

- 1 byte is equivalent to a single character on the keyboard.
- 1 KB (one kilobyte) is 1024 bytes. To make it easier, think of it as about 1000 bytes.
- 1 MB (one megabyte) is 1024 kilobytes. Think of it as about one million bytes.
- 1 GB (one gigabyte) is 1024 megabytes. Think of it as about 1000 megabytes.

Random access memory (RAM)

These chips are from the main memory of a computer.

A computer has a main memory, called random access memory (RAM), which is usually measured in megabytes. Programs have to be in the main memory before they can be used on the computer. This memory can only remember data while the computer is switched on. When it is switched off all the data are lost.

Floppy disk

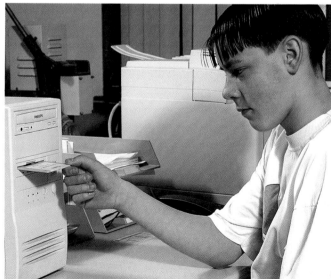

You can use a floppy disk to store data or programs.

The floppy disk goes into the smaller slot in your computer.

Floppy disks can be used to store small amounts of data or programs. They come in various sizes but the most common are shown in the table.

Name	Computer	Capacity
Double density	PC	720 KB
High density	PC	1440 KB (1.44 MB)
Double density	Acorn RISC OS	800 KB
High density	Acorn RISC OS	1600 KB (1.6 MB)

Floppy disks, and hence the data on the disks, can be passed from one computer to another. Some kinds of computers can only read certain kinds of disks. For example, PCs can only read PC disks, but Acorn RISC computers can read both Acorn disks and PC disks.

Floppy disks are the slowest way of storing and retrieving data. When you put the disk into the floppy disk drive on your computer, and request some data from it, the disk starts to revolve. It must come up to speed before it can start sending data to the computer.

Floppy disks are usually used to store programs, text, small pictures and short sounds. Movies and sound take up a lot of storage space, so floppy disks are not suitable for storing information like this.

Hard disks

The hard disk in this computer processor box is in the black casing on the left.

Most computers nowadays contain a **hard disk**. This is a high capacity disk that is fitted to the inside of the main processor box. It is not normally removable. The size of the hard disk is measured in megabytes or gigabytes.

The hard disk is constantly revolving and so stores and retrieves data very quickly. A hard disk has a big enough capacity to store programs, text, pictures, animation, movies and sound.

Compact disks (CD-ROMs)

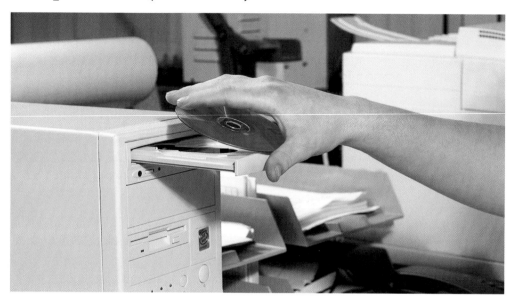

Compact disks store more than just music – in computers they are used to store everything from programs to pictures.

CD-ROM stands for Compact Disk-Read Only Memory. With computers, CD-ROMs are used as portable hard disks on which nothing new can be recorded. They usually have a capacity of 600 MB, and are slower than a hard disk.

The main advantage of a CD-ROM is that it can store a large amount of data in a small space and it is portable. Of course, you must have a computer with a CD-ROM drive to use a CD-ROM disk. Unlike the data on both floppy and hard disks, which is stored magnetically, the data stored on a CD-ROM is read using a laser beam.

A CD-ROM can store programs, text, pictures, animation, movies and sound.

Zip disks

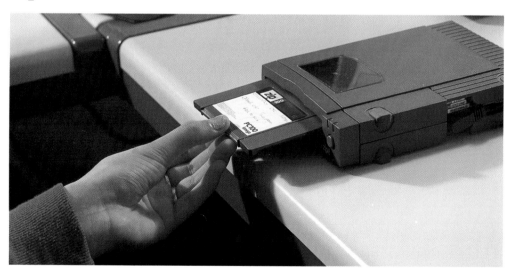

Many people use zip disks to make back-up copies of work they have done using the hard disk.

Zip disks are medium-capacity storage devices. Most can store up to 100 MB of data. Some zip drives can plug into the printer socket on the computer. This makes a zip disk a very portable medium-capacity storage device.

Output from a computer

Screen

The most obvious way of seeing what a computer is doing is to look at the **screen**. The screen is sometimes known as a **visual display unit** (VDU) or a **monitor**. The quality of the screen is measured in dots-per-inch. The more dots there are on the screen in every inch, the more detailed the picture can be.

The quality of the graphics you see on screen is better if your monitor has more dots-per-inch.

Printer

The printer is a way of producing a permanent record of your work. The paper that comes out of the printer is known as **hard copy**. There are several types of printer.

A **dot-matrix printer** produces an image on the paper by firing metal pins at an inked ribbon. Where the ribbon hits the paper, it leaves a printed mark. They are quite noisy machines and relatively slow, but they are very cheap to buy. They can use either black or coloured ribbons, which are also very cheap to buy.

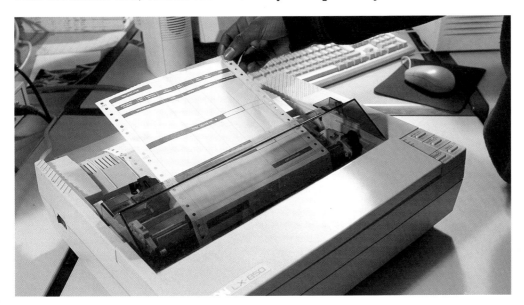

Dot-matrix printers are cheap, but they do not produce high quality images. They are used by supermarkets to print barcodes.

Ink-jet printers produce an image by spraying ink on the paper. They are very quiet and are generally faster than dot-matrix printers. They can use either black-only cartridges, or cartridges containing black with a set of three different colours. The inks mix to produce a complete range of different colours. Ink-jet printers can produce very high quality images. However, they are quite expensive to run because the ink cartridges run out quickly and are costly to replace.

Ink-jet printers are very popular for home use, because they are quite small and quick, and produce good quality printouts.

Like ink-jets, **laser printers** produce an image on the paper a sheet at a time. They operate in a similar way to photocopiers. They are very quiet, generally very fast and produce a very high quality printout, but they are expensive to buy and run. They can either print in black and white or in colour. Colour laser printers are usually very expensive.

Laser printers produce the best quality images, but they are larger than ink-jets.

Speakers

Audio speakers can be connected to a computer so that you can hear noises, words or music produced by the computer. They can be loudspeakers, or personal headphones so that other people in the room cannot hear the sound. Not all computers can produce good quality sound. Some may need to have a piece of electronics known as a **sound card** added to them.

Floor robots

You can use a computer to **control** the movements of an object on the screen. In a similar way, you can control the movements of real objects such as floor turtles and buggies. Using a few simple commands, these devices can be made to move in any direction (see page 49). Turtles and buggies are sometimes referred to as **floor robots**.

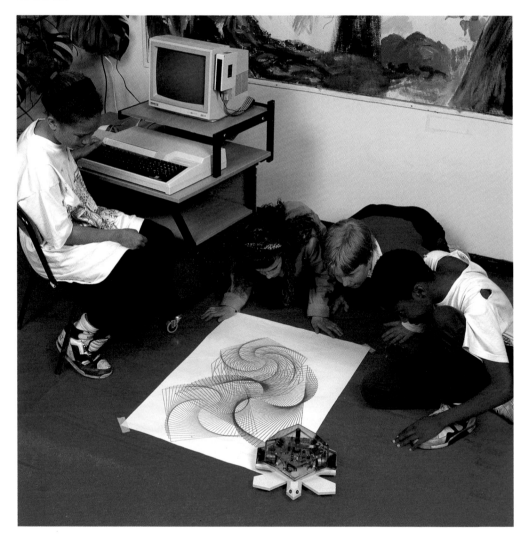

Floor turtles like this one can be controlled using a program written in a programming language called Logo (see page 50).

Plotter

A plotter is a device that can draw lines on a sheet of paper. Plotters usually work by moving a pen in a holder over a fixed piece of paper. The pen can be moved, raised and lowered as required by the program that is controlling the plotter.

Input to a computer
Keyboard

A standard computer keyboard has a similar layout to a typewriter keyboard.

The keyboard is the most obvious form of input. It is used for typing characters into the computer.

Mouse

The mouse contains a small ball that rotates when you move it across a flat surface.

The **mouse** is a device that you hold in your hand and slide over a flat surface, to control the pointer on the computer screen. The mouse might have one, two or three buttons on top, depending on the type of computer you are using. Clicking the button makes some action happen, for example, choosing something from a screen **menu**. You can also use the mouse to control the pointer to draw on the screen.

Joystick

Joysticks are often used when playing games on the computer.

A joystick operates like the joystick in an aeroplane. Moving the joystick in any direction makes the pointer on the screen move in the same way. It usually has one, or two, buttons so that other actions can be taken.

Concept keyboard

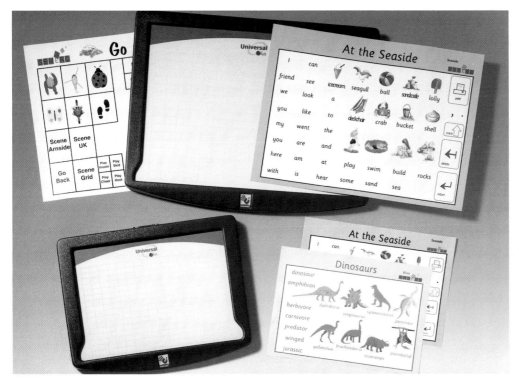

Concept keyboards or overlay keyboards have a variety of uses.

A **concept keyboard** is a large flat surface that is divided into squares, often 128 squares. When you press one of the squares, an action occurs on the screen. A block of squares can be grouped together so that pressing anywhere on a large area will cause something to happen. A computer program controls what happens when you press the concept keyboard. For example, the computer program could be set up so that pressing an area with a picture of a duck on it makes the word 'duck' appear on the screen.

Concept keyboards, or overlay keyboards, are used in fast-food restaurants and many school canteens. The keyboards are attached to the tills. The squares on the keyboard each represent an item of food, so the price of every item does not have to be keyed in. The keyboard also has numbers so that the number of items of food that have been sold can be entered.

Graphics tablet

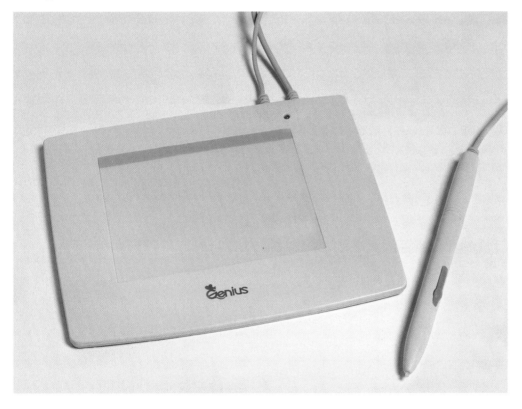

Using a graphics tablet feels almost like drawing on paper.

A graphics tablet is a flat surface on which the user can draw using a special pen. The shape you draw on the tablet is transferred to the computer screen. This is an easy way of transferring pictures to the computer since many people find it difficult to 'draw on the screen' using a mouse.

Scanner

Scanners and **digital cameras** are used to transfer pictures to a computer. Once the pictures are in the computer you can alter them or add them to other documents. Digital cameras are operated by pressing a button to take a picture. The picture is then stored in the camera. Motorised flat-bed scanners are quite accurate. Some scanners and digital cameras can only transfer pictures in black and white, but most can produce colour images on screen.

Scanners and digital
cameras turn pictures into
a form of data that the
computer can understand.

Communicating

One of the main world-wide uses of computers is to communicate information. **Word processors** and **desktop publishing** packages allow you to create text, to arrange and style it on the page, and to print it. **Computer aided design** packages can be used to show simple graphic ideas or detailed drawings.

There are also many other ways to communicate information using computers, such as music, animation, multimedia, music scores, cartoons and world wide web pages.

What is a word processor?

A word processor is a computer program that allows you to enter **text**, alter it and **save** it. You can also print out your work. There are many other operations that the word processor can perform, such as making the words bigger, changing the style of the letters, and lining up the edges of the writing. You can make the text **bold**, underlined or in *italics*. Many word processors can also import pictures, such as **clip art** or even **graphics** that you have created yourself.

There will be a word processing program on the computers you use in school. This book cannot train you to use the features of your particular word processing program, because there are many different word processors. Instead we shall look at the operations performed by all word processors.

Loading the word processor

Before you start, the word processing program needs to be loaded from the hard disk into the main memory of your computer. You normally do this by double clicking the left mouse button while you are pointing at the icon for the word processor on the screen.

Entering text

Once the word processor is loaded, you can start to type your text. You should, of course, have thought about what you want to write before you start (i.e. you should have planned your work). In the example shown here, the piece of text is about the **Internet**.

The Internet is a large collection of computers all over the world that can be accessed from a home computer. To get into the Internet, you need some software and a modem connected between your computer and the telephone line. The modem turns the output from your computer into signals that the telephone system can understand.

There is a flashing straight line that shows you where the letters will go when you press the keys on the keyboard. This is known as the **cursor** (or **caret**, or arrow).

It is possible that something will go wrong and you might lose all the work you have done. So once you have entered your text you should *save it straight away*.

Saving your work

Ask your teacher how you save a piece of text in your particular word processor. The saved work is known as a **document**. Every document you save is given a name so that you can identify it again later.

You might save by clicking on a button at the top of the screen. This button often has a picture of a floppy disk on it.

You will be asked to give your work a name. Do not give it your own name, because you can only use that once! Choose a name that has something to do with what you have typed, to remind you what the document contains.

You can save your work in a **directory** or folder, which keeps documents together a bit like a real folder. Remember in which directory you saved your work, so that you can find it again easily.

Loading your work

If you have closed your document, but now want to do some more work on it, you will need to load it into the main computer memory again. Ask your teacher how you load your document.

To load your document, you might have to go to a menu at the top of the screen and choose **Open** from a list. This term means that you want to load a document from the disk, to change or edit it. You will see a window on the screen showing directories and documents. Look in the directory in which you saved your document. Highlight the document by clicking the left button once with the pointer on its name, and then click on OK.

To load your work on other makes of computer you might have to start by finding the directory in which you saved your document. Point at the document icon and double click the left mouse button. This should load the word processor with your document.

In either case the document will be loaded into the word processor exactly as it was when you last saved it.

Editing your document

You might want to change some of the text in your document or correct some spelling errors. Use the pointer to position the cursor in front of the word you want to change and click the left mouse button. You can now type at this position. You could also use the **backspace** key to delete text. On the keyboard, the backspace key is the long key with a left-pointing arrow, to the left of the Insert key.

If you put the cursor at the beginning of the text, you can type a heading for your work. Press **Enter** twice at the end of the heading to create a blank line between the heading and the text that follows.

The Internet

The Internet is a large collection of computers all over the world that can be accessed from a home computer. To get into the Internet, you need some software and a modem connected between your computer and the telephone line. The modem turns the output from your computer into signals that the telephone system can understand.

Highlighting a piece of your text

If you want to do something to a part of your text, say the heading, you must **highlight** it first. You do this by placing the mouse pointer where you want to start the highlighting, pressing the left mouse button and keeping it pressed, then dragging the pointer to where you want the highlighting to end. The highlighted area will change to white writing on black instead of black writing on white. Once the area is highlighted, let go of the mouse button.

You can then choose an action to carry out on the highlighted text. The actions may be on buttons at the top of the screen, such as:

I	italic	changes the text to *italics* (slanted writing)
B	bold	changes the text to **bold** (heavy print)
U	underline	underlines the text

In the example below, the heading has been made bold.

The Internet

The Internet is a large collection of computers all over the world that can be accessed from a home computer. To get into the Internet, you need some software and a modem connected between your computer and the telephone line. The modem turns the output from your computer into signals that the telephone system can understand.

Justifying the text

If you just start to type in a new document, the piece of text you produce may have a straight left edge and a ragged right edge. Some people like the writing to have straight edges on both sides. This is known as justifying the text (or **justification**). You do this by highlighting the paragraph you want to justify, and then clicking on a button at the top of the screen. There are usually buttons such as:

	left	makes the left edge straight and the right edge ragged
	centre	makes the whole text centred about the middle of the page
	right	makes the right edge straight and the left edge ragged
	justify	makes both edges straight

In the example below, the heading has been centred and the text has been justified.

The Internet

The Internet is a large collection of computers all over the world that can be accessed from a home computer. To get into the Internet, you need some software and a modem connected between your computer and the telephone line. The modem turns the output from your computer into signals that the telephone system can understand.

Changing the font

The shape of the letters is called the **font**. Fonts are given names like Homerton, Helvetica, Arial, Ghost and so on. Here are some different fonts.

This is in a font called Arial.

This is in a font called Courier

This is in a font called Times New Roman

THIS IS IN A FONT CALLED DESDEMONA

This is in a font called Matura MT Script

This is in a font called Comic Sans MS

Your computer will have its own set of fonts installed. Highlight the text you want to change and then choose the new font.

Changing the size of the font

You can also control the size of the font using the button bar at the top of the screen. The size of the font is shown by a number measured in points. Highlight the text you want to change and then choose the new size number.

This Arial at 8 point

This Arial at 10 point

This Arial at 12 point

This Arial at 18 point

This Arial at 24 point

The text in the example below is in Times New Roman at 11 point.

The Internet

The Internet is a large collection of computers all over the world that can be accessed from a home computer. To get into the Internet, you need some software and a modem connected between your computer and the telephone line. The modem turns the output from your computer into signals that the telephone system can understand.

Inserting a picture

Most word processors will allow you to insert a picture into the text. The picture could be one you have drawn yourself or one which you have taken from a clip art disk. The way you insert the picture can be quite different on different word processors. Ask your teacher how you should insert a picture.

You may have to select Insert Picture from a menu at the top of the screen. You will then see a window from which you can select your picture. You may have to re-size the picture once it appears on the screen.

You may have to create a frame by clicking on the Create Frame button at the top of the screen. Once you have drawn the frame you can drag and drop the picture into it (see 'Moving a picture', below).

In the example, a picture of a modem has been added to illustrate the text.

The Internet

The Internet is a large collection of computers all over the world that can be accessed from a home computer. To get into the Internet, you need some software and a modem connected between your computer and the telephone line. The modem turns the output from your computer into signals that the telephone system can understand.

Moving a picture

If you are not happy with the position of your picture you can move it. Place the pointer inside the picture frame and press the left mouse button. Now, keeping the mouse button down, you can move or 'drag' the picture around. When the picture is where you want it, you can 'drop' it by letting go of the mouse button.

Printing a document

You can print your document any time you like. There will usually be a button at the top of the screen with a picture of a printer on it. Click on this button. What appears on the paper should be exactly what you have created on the screen.

Exercise

Change the following text according to the instructions below. When you have carried out each instruction, use your new text for the next action.

Book Review

This chapter shows that George and Lennie are wandering workers who, unusually, like to travel together. They have very different characters. Lennie is a rather large man, but acts as a child might act. The author compares him to various animals in order to emphasise his simple-mindedness. For instance, he often calls Lennie's hands paws.

George in many ways is Lennie's exact opposite. He is a small clever man with 'restless eyes and sharp, strong features'. He is almost always thinking about Lennie.

In many ways George and Lennie have a brother-like relationship. Lennie relies on George for the simplest of things and often mimics George's actions.

George and Lennie have a dream. George's dream is slightly different to Lennie's. George wants to own a ranch and live well, but Lennie simply wants some pet rabbits, and he is forever asking George to tell him the dream of the ranch and the rabbits, like a very small child.

---

1 Place the title in the centre.
2 Change the font of the title to a font of your choice.
3 Change the size of the title.
4 Put the title in bold.
5 Justify all of the body of the text.
6 Find the names George and Lennie. Put all the names into italics.
7 Find a piece of clip art that you think goes with the text. Insert it into the text.

What is a DTP package?

A DTP (desktop publishing) package is a computer program that allows you to position text and pictures on the screen, and then to print the pages out. The text could have been created using a word processor or created inside the DTP package. Pictures and text are usually kept in **frames** on the screen, which can be moved to any position you like as you design the page.

Using a DTP package

DTP packages are used to design the pages of almost all illustrated books, magazines and newspapers these days.

Desktop publishing programs have traditionally been used to create magazines, newspapers, brochures, reports, manuals, advertisements, school magazines and so on. They were also particularly suited to presenting work in columns. However, nowadays word processors have become so advanced that they can often perform many of the functions of a DTP package. If the word processor in your school can be used to arrange text and pictures as you like on a page, then it may not be necessary to use a separate DTP program.

What is a CAD package?

A CAD (computer aided design) or graphics package is one that enables you to draw designs on the screen, and then to print them out. These designs can be very accurate engineering drawings for industry or simple sketches to see what a design might look like. Often these designs are created as front views and end views. The computer can then produce a three-dimensional image of the object and let you see what it really looks like.

This is the front view of a house that has been designed using a CAD package.

Computers are particularly suited to designing objects that have to be built and used. They can be used to help design all kinds of useful objects, such as cars, aircraft, buildings and packaging.

Using a CAD package

A CAD package allows you to create an object and then to change that object's size, position and colour.

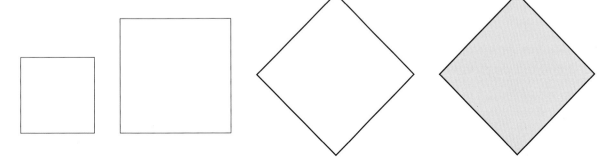

Using a CAD package you can draw a square, make it bigger, turn it round and colour it in.

The CAD program in your school should have these main features:

- You can alter each shape you create (for example, a line, rectangle or circle) without affecting the rest of the drawing.
- You can place objects over or underneath each other.
- You can shade areas in a variety of styles.
- You can adjust the sizes of objects.
- You can store a bank of standard objects and use them in various designs.
- You can add text to your designs.
- You can print out your designs.

Your teacher will show you how to use the CAD program in your school. At first you should try to design a simple object so that you can get used to the program.

Exercises

1 Design a battery symbol for a sticker to be placed in a radio, to show how the batteries fit.

2 Design a window frame for a living room.

3 Design the front view of a washing machine.

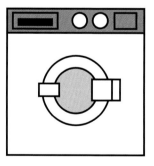

4 Design the front view of a microwave oven.

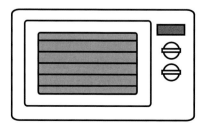

5 Design a label for sticking on the front of a music video tape. The label should contain:

- the title of the video
- the title of one of the songs
- an outer edge with curved corners
- a picture of the performer

The picture of the performer might be taken from a scanned image from a magazine or newspaper, or can simply be a piece of clip art.

Evaluation of a communication package

When you have used a word processor or a CAD program for a while, you will have an idea of how useful it is in doing what you want it to do.

To evaluate a program, you should think about a number of things.

For a word processor

1 How good or bad was the word processor for editing text?
2 How easy or hard was it to change the look of the text to bold, italic and so on?
3 How easy or hard was it to change the size or font of the text?
4 How easy or hard was it to move the text to a different position on the screen?
5 How easy or hard was it to import pictures?

For a CAD or graphics package

1 How easy or hard was it to draw shapes, such as squares, rectangles and circles?
2 How easy or hard was it to import clip art?
3 How easy or hard was it to change colours?
4 How easy or hard was it to alter the picture once you had drawn it?

In an evaluation, do not talk about whether you enjoyed doing the project. Always make remarks about what you were doing, and *not* how you felt about it.

Handling Data

What is handling data?

Information handling has been around for hundreds of years. Ever since writing was first developed people have been storing information on parchment or paper. To find information, you had to search through the papers. Later, papers were grouped together to form books. If books are organised into some sort of order it can make the searching much easier. To find information in a library, you can go to a catalogue that is in alphabetical order and find a reference to a book containing the information you want. You can then go to the shelves and find the actual book. Then you can look in the index of the book to find the page with the information you need. Nowadays, this kind of searching can be done by computer using a **data handling program**. However, just as there must be books in the library for you to find what you want, there must be information in the computer for the program to search. This information is in the form of a **database**.

Databases

A database is a collection of data, all of which has some connection. For example, data about students in a school is held on a computer database in the school office. A set of data is stored about each student. This is known as the student's **record**. Each record is split up into a number of sections, such as the student's name, sex, address and so on. Each of these sections is known as a **field**. The complete set of records about all the children is known as a database. The individual records can be held as separate files on the disk or as a single file.

Student Record

Name:	Smith
Forenames:	John
Sex:	Male
Address:	150 Great South Road, Hatfield, Hertfordshire
Postcode:	AL9 8QQ
Date of Birth:	22-11-1985

This is the record for one student. The record has six fields. It is part of a student database that contains many such records, one for each student in the school.

You can think of a database as a table, with a set of records (the rows) divided into fields (the columns). The following example database shows some information about a number of people, taken from a survey. Each person's hometown is where he or she was born.

The first row contains the field names that refer to each column.

Surname	Forename	Age	Sex	Hometown
Chapman	Mary	35	Female	Watford
Smith	Alexander	27	Male	Leeds
Jones	Harvey	56	Male	Manchester
Evans	David	34	Male	Swansea
Smith	Joanna	23	Female	Luton
Carter	Fred	65	Male	London
Conner	Renee	28	Female	Stevenage
Law	Lucy	30	Female	Leeds
Smith	Kevin	37	Male	Cambridge
Leick	Heidi	25	Female	Oxford
O'Leary	Carole	21	Female	London
Gynn	Billy	19	Male	Poole

In this example the database is very small (only 12 records), so any questions that you might use the computer to answer can just as easily be done by simply looking at it.

For example, you might want to ask 'What is the hometown of Fred Carter?' You can just look down the table, find Fred Carter and read across to his hometown (London).

However, imagine trying to do this for a database of 20 000 records. It could be done, but it would take a great deal of time for every single search. For this amount of data you need to use a database stored on a computer if you are to get your results in a reasonable time.

The data in the example comes from a survey. In this case, the ages of the people were written down. In databases about people, such as school records, the dates of birth are recorded. This is because the dates of birth never change. If the ages were recorded they would all be wrong after one year.

Types of data

There are a number of ways in which databases can store data. The main two ways are as **string data** (text data) or as **numeric data**.

String data

A piece of string data is often just a word, or several words, such as:

- a surname   for example, Smith
- an address   for example, 150 Great South Road, Hatfield, Hertfordshire
- a code   for example, M (meaning male)

String data are sometimes called text data, because they contain text.

Numeric data

A piece of numeric data is a number. A number can represent anything that needs a value:

- an age   for example, 27
- a salary   for example, 12 000
- a school year   for example, 10

You do not write any unit value with the number. For example, a distance of 12 kilometres would be entered in the field of a database as 12. Either there would be another field for the units (km), or all the fields (all the data in that column) would be measured in the same units so there would be no need to store this information.

Data handling programs

Your school will have a data handling program on the computers you use. This book cannot train you to use the features of your particular data handling program, because there are many different ones. Instead we shall look at the main operations performed by all data handling programs.

Data handling programs can be used to search huge amounts of information quickly and easily.

Loading the data handling program

Before you start, the data handling program needs to be loaded from the hard disk into the main memory of your computer, or RAM (see page 4). You normally do this by double clicking the left mouse button while you are pointing at the icon for the data handling program on the screen.

Searching

To find information from the database you must be able to **search** it. This is called a **query** or a **find** in some data handling programs. The way you do this will depend on your particular database. You will usually have to click on a button at the top of the screen.

There are three things that the data handling program must know to find a particular item:

- **which field to search** – you must tell the data handling program which column you want to look down
- **what to look for** – you must tell the program what you are looking for. This is often called the **value**
- **relationship** – you have to specify what **relationship** you want to look for

It might be that you are searching for all the people named Smith, or everyone who is over 30 years of age. In these cases the relationships would be:

Field	Relationship	Data to look for (value)
Name	'identical to'	Smith
Age	'greater than'	30

Using our example database (see page 25), you could perform a search for someone whose surname is Carter. You need to tell the computer the following:

Field	Relationship	Data to look for
Surname	'identical to'	Carter

The search should produce this result:

Surname	Forename	Age	Sex	Hometown
Carter	Fred	65	Male	London

There are many relationships that you can use, as the following table shows. These relationships allow you to search for large groups of data.

Type of data	Relationship	Meaning	Examples
Text	'identical to'	Find all the data that is *exactly* the same as the value	value is the same as London
Text	'starts with'	Find all the data that start with a particular letter or group of letters	value starts with A value starts with Let
Text	'ends with'	Find all the data that end with a particular letter or group of letters	value ends with g value ends with ing
Text	'contains'	Find all the data that contain a particular letter or group of letters	value contains g value contains math
Text	'comes after'	Find all the data that come after a letter or group of letters in the alphabet	value comes after F value comes after Fig
Text	'comes before'	Find all the data that come before a letter or group of letters in the alphabet	value comes before F value comes before Fig
Numeric	=	The value must be *exactly* the same as the number	value = 12
Numeric	>	The value must be greater than the number	value > 12
Numeric	<	The value must be less than the number	value < 12
Numeric	<>	The value must be different to the number	value <> 12
Numeric	$\geq$	The value must be greater than or exactly the same as the number	value $\geq$ 12
Numeric	$\leq$	The value must be less than or exactly the same as the number	value $\leq$ 12

Example 1

Find all the females in the example database (see page 25).

Field	Relationship	Data to look for
Sex	'identical to'	Female

The search should produce a result such as:

Surname	Forename	Age	Sex	Hometown
Chapman	Mary	35	Female	Watford
Smith	Joanna	23	Female	Luton
Conner	Renee	28	Female	Stevenage
Law	Lucy	30	Female	Leeds
Leick	Heidi	25	Female	Oxford
O'Leary	Carole	21	Female	London

Example 2

In the example database, find all the people whose surnames begin with C.

Field	Relationship	Data to look for
Surname	'starts with'	C

The search should produce a result such as:

Surname	Forename	Age	Sex	Hometown
Chapman	Mary	35	Female	Watford
Carter	Fred	65	Male	London
Conner	Renee	28	Female	Stevenage

Example 3

In the example database, find all the people who are over 30.

Field	Relationship	Data to look for
Age	>	30

The search should produce a result such as:

Surname	Forename	Age	Sex	Hometown
Chapman	Mary	35	Female	Watford
Jones	Harvey	56	Male	Manchester
Evans	David	34	Male	Swansea
Carter	Fred	65	Male	London
Smith	Kevin	37	Male	Cambridge

Combining searches

You can search for more than one item at once. This is known as a complex search. There are two ways in which data handling programs allow you to do this, depending on the program that you have.

Method 1

The first method involves two stages:

1 Search the database for the first value you want to be true.
2 Search the results of the first search for the second value you want to be true.

Example 4

Suppose that you want to find all the females under 30, in the example database (see page 25).

The first search to make is:

Field	Relationship	Data to look for
Age	<	30

This results in:

Surname	Forename	Age	Sex	Hometown
Smith	Alexander	27	Male	Leeds
Smith	Joanna	23	Female	Luton
Conner	Renee	28	Female	Stevenage
Leick	Heidi	25	Female	Oxford
O'Leary	Carole	21	Female	London
Gynn	Billy	19	Male	Poole

The second search based on these results is:

Field	Relationship	Data to look for
Sex	'identical to'	Female

This results in:

Surname	Forename	Age	Sex	Hometown
Smith	Joanna	23	Female	Luton
Conner	Renee	28	Female	Stevenage
Leick	Heidi	25	Female	Oxford
O'Leary	Carole	21	Female	London

These two searches can be done in either order and will produce the same final results.

If this two-stage method of searching is used, there must be a way of going back to be able to search the complete database afterwards. There is usually an item on a menu that will reset the data back to its original state.

Method 2

Using the second method, you ask the computer to perform both searches at once. Only when both are true is a match made.

Field	Relationship	Data to look for
Age	<	30
and		
Sex	'identical to'	Female

This immediately results in the final table produced by Method 1.

Saving your work

Ask your teacher how to save your database. Every database you save is given a name so that you can identify it again.

To save, you may have to click on a button at the top of the screen. This button often has a picture of a floppy disk on it.

You will be asked to give your work a name. Do not give it your own name, because you can only use that once! Choose a name that has something to do with your database, to remind you what data it contains.

You can save your work in a directory or folder, which keeps documents together a bit like a real folder. Remember in which directory you saved your work, so that you can find it again easily.

Be careful when you save!

You must take care not to destroy the original database. If you click on save, you might save only the final results of your searches, and lose all the original data. Some databases will not let you overwrite the original data in this way, but to make sure, give your final database a different name to the original database.

Sorting the data

It is easier to find data if it is in some kind of order. The order can be alphabetic or numeric.

There may be a button on the top of the screen that will start the sorting. You will need to tell the data handling program two things:

1 which field you wish to use for sorting
2 in which order you want the data arranged

If it is string data (words) then you might want the sorting to be alphabetic or perhaps reverse alphabetic.

If it is numeric data (numbers) the sorting can be done with the numbers increasing or decreasing.

Example 5

Sort the original database (see page 25) into alphabetic order using the Surname field.

Surname	Forename	Age	Sex	Hometown
Carter	Fred	65	Male	London
Chapman	Mary	35	Female	Watford
Conner	Renee	28	Female	Stevenage
Evans	David	34	Male	Swansea
Gynn	Billy	19	Male	Poole
Jones	Harvey	56	Male	Manchester
Law	Lucy	30	Female	Leeds
Leick	Heidi	25	Female	Oxford
O'Leary	Carole	21	Female	London
Smith	Alexander	27	Male	Leeds
Smith	Joanna	23	Female	Luton
Smith	Kevin	37	Male	Cambridge

Example 6

Sort the original database into age order using the Age field.

Surname	Forename	Age	Sex	Hometown
Gynn	Billy	19	Male	Poole
O'Leary	Carole	21	Female	London
Smith	Joanna	23	Female	Luton
Leick	Heidi	25	Female	Oxford
Smith	Alexander	27	Male	Leeds
Conner	Renee	28	Female	Stevenage
Law	Lucy	30	Female	Leeds
Evans	David	34	Male	Swansea
Chapman	Mary	35	Female	Watford
Smith	Kevin	37	Male	Cambridge
Jones	Harvey	56	Male	Manchester
Carter	Fred	65	Male	London

If you now carry out a search on the reordered database, the results will also be sorted in the same way.

Exercise

Using this database of monarchs (kings and queens), answer the following questions.

Monarch	Born	Crowned	Years in reign	How died (or why reign ended)	Age died	Family
William the Conqueror	1025	1066	21	Murdered	60	Norman
William Rufus	1056	1087	13	Killed when hunting	43	Norman
Henry I	1070	1100	35	Old age	67	Norman
Stephen	1096	1135	19	Old age	50	Norman
Henry II	1133	1154	35	Old age	56	Plantagenet
Richard I	1157	1189	10	Killed in battle	42	Plantagenet
John	1166	1199	17	Old age	50	Plantagenet
Henry III	1206	1216	56	Old age	65	Plantagenet
Edward I	1239	1272	35	Old age	68	Plantagenet
Edward II	1284	1307	20	Murdered	43	Plantagenet
Edward III	1312	1327	50	Old age	65	Plantagenet
Richard II	1366	1377	22	Died in prison	34	Plantagenet
Henry IV	1366	1399	13	Illness	47	Plantagenet-Lancaster
Henry V	1388	1413	9	Camp fever	34	Plantagenet-Lancaster
Henry VI	1421	1422	39	Murdered	49	Plantagenet-Lancaster
Edward IV	1442	1461	22	Over indulgence	41	Plantagenet-York
Edward V	1470	1483	0.3	Murdered	13	Plantagenet-York
Richard III	1452	1483	2	Killed in battle	32	Plantagenet-York
Henry VII	1457	1485	24	Illness	53	Tudor
Henry VIII	1491	1509	38	Old age	56	Tudor
Edward VI	1537	1547	6	Illness	16	Tudor
Mary I	1516	1553	5	Illness	43	Tudor
Jane Grey	1537	1553	0	Executed	17	Tudor
Elizabeth I	1533	1558	45	Old age	69	Tudor
James I	1566	1603	22	Old age	59	Stuart
Charles I	1600	1648	24	Beheaded	48	Stuart
Charles II	1630	1660	36	Old age	55	Stuart
James II	1633	1685	4	(Deposed)	68	Stuart
William (and Mary)	1650	1689	13	Old age	51	Stuart-Orange
Anne	1665	1702	12	Old age	49	Stuart
George I	1660	1714	13	Old age	67	Hanover
George II	1683	1727	33	Old age	77	Hanover
George III	1738	1760	6	Old age	81	Hanover
George IV	1762	1820	10	Old age	67	Hanover
William IV	1765	1830	7	Old age	71	Hanover
Victoria	1819	1837	64	Old age	81	Hanover
Edward VII	1841	1901	9	Old age	68	Saxe-Coburg
George V	1865	1910	26	Old age	70	Windsor
Edward VIII	1894	1936	0.9	(Abdicated)	68	Windsor
George VI	1895	1936	16	Old age	56	Windsor
Elizabeth II	1926	1952				Windsor

1 Which monarchs died of old age? (Hint: search for 'Old age' in the 'How died' column.)
2 Which monarchs were crowned last century? (Hint: search the 'Crowned' field for a date greater or equal to 1900.)
3 Which monarch reigned for the longest length of time? (Hint: sort the 'Years in reign' column.)
4 Which monarch reigned for the shortest length of time?
5 Which monarchs were executed?
6 Which monarchs belonged to the Tudor family?

Printing your database

You can print your database any time you like. There will be a button at the top of the screen with a picture of a printer on it. Click on this button.

You will have a choice of ways of printing the data:

1 You can choose which field you want to print. You might have done all the searches you need to, and now be interested in only the name of each person and his or her hometown. In this case, you would ask the data handling program to print only Surname, Forename, Hometown.
2 You may be able to choose how you want the data to appear. It could be in columns, as in all the examples above. It could be as single records (see page 24).

Other types of databases

In this chapter, you have only looked at the type of database where the data is divided into records and fields. Other types of databases exist that produce very different output.

Encyclopaedias

Encyclopaedias are often found on CD-ROMs. The actions you perform on them are just the same as on the databases you have looked at so far.

Loading

There will be an icon for you to double click on once the CD-ROM is in the CD-ROM drive. This will load the encyclopaedia into the main memory of the computer. A front screen will usually appear to tell you what it is.

Searching

There will be a button to click on that will start the search procedure. A box will appear on the screen, into which you type what you want to search for.

Refining your search

You can take all the results of your search and search them again, looking for different values this time, to produce a new, more specific set of results.

Saving
Once you find what you are looking for, you can save what you see on the screen as a piece of text. You could then load the text into a word processor.

Printing
Once you find what you are looking for, you can print what you see on the screen.

Types of data
Usually, all you can search for is string data (words), even if it looks like a number. However there are some different types of data you can find. These include pictures, sound, animation and movies.

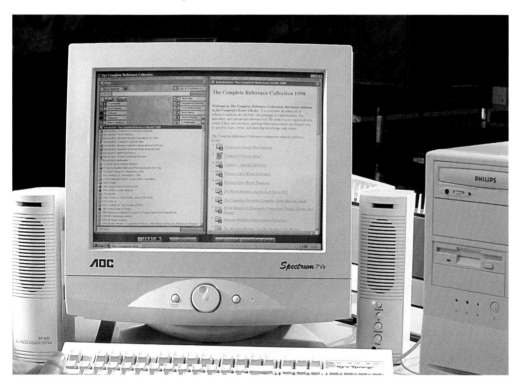

CD-ROM encyclopaedias are basically huge databases that you can search for all kinds of information.

Internet
The Internet is a collection of computers around the world from which you can obtain data. Again, the actions for using the Internet to find data are similar to what you have already learned.

Loading
There will be an icon for you to double click to access the Internet. The part of the Internet that you will have access to is known as the world wide web.

Searching
You will need to access a search engine to find what you are looking for. There are several search engines you can use. Some of the most popular are called Alta Vista, Lycos and Hotbot. Once you have the front screen of the search engine in front of you, there will be a box into which you type what you want to search for.

Refining your search

Using some search engines, you can take all the results of your search and search them again, looking for a different value this time, to produce a new, more specific set of results. In others, you can refine your search by entering more than one value in the search box.

Saving

Once you find what you are looking for, you can save what you see on the screen as a piece of text. You could then load the text into a word processor.

Printing

Once you find what you are looking for, you can print what you see on the screen.

Types of data

As for encyclopaedias, all you can usually search for is string data (words), even if it looks like a number. However, there are some different types of data you can find, including pictures, sound, animation and movies.

Evaluation of a data handling program

When you have used a data handling program for a while, you will have an idea of how useful it is in doing what you want it to do.

To evaluate a data handling program, you should think about a number of things.

1 How much faster was it to use the program instead of doing all the searches by hand?
2 How good or bad was the program at sorting the data?
3 How easy or hard was it to search the data for what you wanted?
4 How easy or hard was it to refine your search?
5 How easy or hard was it to save your results?
6 How easy or hard was it to print what you wanted?

In an evaluation, do not talk about whether you enjoyed doing the project. Always make remarks about what you were doing, and *not* how you felt about it.

Modelling

What is modelling?

A **model** represents something real. In computer terms, the word modelling means using a computer to represent a real life situation. Often computer models use mathematics to describe how a situation works. You can try out different situations by putting different numbers into the model. This is known as asking 'what if' questions. Using a computer model, you can see how something will turn out before you build it. The model could be created on a **spreadsheet**.

Spreadsheets

Your school will have a spreadsheet program on the computers you use. This book cannot train you to use the features of your particular program, because there are many different ones. Instead we shall look at the main operations performed by all spreadsheet programs.

Spreadsheets are divided into boxes known as **cells**. The columns are referred to by letters, and the rows by numbers. A particular cell is identified by a letter and a number. The letter usually comes first. In the spreadsheet below, the cell that is shaded is cell B5 – the cell in column B and row 5.

	A	B	C	D
1			Answer	
2	5	3	=A2+B2	
3				
4				
5		This is cell B5		
6				
7				
8				
9				
10				

Loading the spreadsheet program

Before you start, the spreadsheet program needs to be loaded from the hard disk into the main memory of your computer. You normally do this by double clicking the left mouse button while you are pointing at the icon for the spreadsheet program on the screen.

Inserting an item

Cells can contain several different types of items. For example, an item could be a word, a number or a formula. To insert an item into a cell you first need to point to the cell and then click the left mouse button. You then just start typing.

Text

In the spreadsheet on page 37, cell C1 contains a word. Cell B5 contains several words. When you type into a cell, if you start the typing with a letter the computer assumes that the item is going to be text. You can use text to enter headings and labels to make your spreadsheet easier for someone else to understand.

Number

In the example, cell A2 and cell B2 each contain a number. These numbers are going to be used to carry out calculations. When you type into a cell, if you start the typing with a number the computer assumes that the cell is going to contain a number.

Formula

Cell C2 in the example spreadsheet contains a **formula**. This is a calculation that is to be done using the numbers from other cells in the spreadsheet. To tell the spreadsheet that you are going to enter a formula, you must start typing with an equals (=) sign.

The formula in C2 is A2+B2. This means that the number in A2 is added to the number in B2, and the answer appears in C2. In this case, the answer is 8, so 8 is the number you will see in C2. You do not normally see the formula after you have typed it. You only see the result of the calculation.

If you change the number in B2 from 3 to 4 then the number in C2 will automatically change to the new result of the calculation, which is 9.

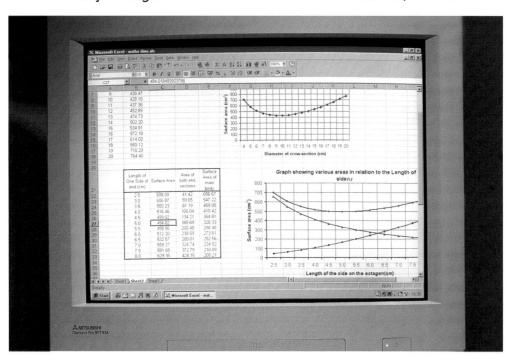

In a spreadsheet model, you can try out different situations by putting in different numbers and seeing how this affects the whole system.

Arithmetic symbols

To perform any arithmetic in a spreadsheet, you type in a formula using the symbols shown in the table below.

	Symbol	Example
Addition	+	A2+C2
Subtraction	–	A2–C2
Multiplication	*	A2*C2
Division	/	A2/C2
Raising to a power	^	A2^3

Using brackets in a formula means that the part in brackets is worked out first. For example, 2*(A2–C2) means that the content of C2 is taken from the content of A2, and then the result is multiplied by 2.

Example

This spreadsheet shows how many miles a person travels each day of the week.

	A	B	C	D
1	Weekly journeys by car			
2				
3	Day	Distance (miles)		
4	Sunday	5		
5	Monday	25		
6	Tuesday	33		
7	Wednesday	27		
8	Thursday	22		
9	Friday	28		
10	Saturday	10		
11	Total	150		

The content of column A is all text. The contents of cells B4 to B10 are numbers. The content of cell B11 is a formula.

The formula in B11 gives us the total for cells B4 to B10. It could be =B4+B5+B6+B7+B8+B9+B10. This is a lot of typing. Think how long the formula would be if the spreadsheet showed the distances travelled on every day of the year – 365 cells to add together!

To make things easier, you can use this special formula: =SUM(B4:B10). This means 'add up all the numbers starting at cell B4 and ending at cell B10'.

Saving your work

Ask your teacher how to save your spreadsheet. Every spreadsheet you save is given a name so that you can identify it again.

To save, you may have to click on a button at the top of the screen. This button often has a picture of a floppy disk on it.

You will be asked to give your work a name. Do not give it your own name, because you can only use that once! Choose a name that has something to do with your spreadsheet, to remind you what data it contains.

You can save your work in a directory or folder, which keeps documents together a bit like a real folder. Remember in which directory you saved your work, so that you can find it again easily.

Loading your work

If you have closed your spreadsheet, but now want to do some more work on it, you will need to load it into the main computer memory again. Ask your teacher how you load your spreadsheet.

To load your spreadsheet, you might have to go to a menu at the top of the screen and choose Open from a list. This term means that you want to load a document from the disk, to change or edit it. You will see a window on the screen showing directories and documents. Look in the directory in which you saved your spreadsheet. Highlight the spreadsheet by clicking the left button once with the pointer on its name, and then click on OK.

To load your work on other makes of computer you might have to start by finding the directory in which you saved your spreadsheet. Point at the document icon and double click the left mouse button. This should load your spreadsheet.

In either case, your work will be loaded into the spreadsheet program exactly as it was when you last saved it.

Changing the numbers

If one of the items in your spreadsheet is wrong, you can change it easily. For instance, in the example spreadsheet (see page 39), if the distance travelled on Tuesday should have been 43 instead of 33, the number in cell B6 can be changed. You simply click on cell B6 and type 43. If you do this, you should notice that the total distance in cell B11 changes to 160 automatically (see opposite). It is this feature that makes spreadsheets very useful for modelling.

Highlighting a part of your spreadsheet

If you want to do something to a part of your spreadsheet, say the title, you must highlight it first. You do this by pointing the mouse pointer at the cell where you want to start the highlighting, pressing the left mouse button and keeping it pressed, then dragging the pointer to the cell where you want the highlighting to end. The area will change to white writing on black instead of black writing on white. Once the area is highlighted let go of the left mouse button.

	A	B	C	D
1	Weekly journeys by car			
2				
3	Day	Distance (miles)		
4	Sunday	5		
5	Monday	25		
6	Tuesday	43		
7	Wednesday	27		
8	Thursday	22		
9	Friday	28		
10	Saturday	10		
11	Total	160		

Changing the type of writing

Once you have highlighted a piece of text, you can choose an action to carry out on it. The actions may be on buttons at the top of the screen. The buttons usually include:

I	italic	changes the text to *italics* (slanted writing)
B	bold	changes the text to **bold** (heavy print)
U	underline	<u>underlines</u> the text

In your spreadsheet, you could make the title and the column headings bold as well as the row that contains the results.

	A	B	C	D
1	**Weekly journeys by car**			
2				
3	**Day**	**Distance (miles)**		
4	Sunday	5		
5	Monday	25		
6	Tuesday	43		
7	Wednesday	27		
8	Thursday	22		
9	Friday	28		
10	Saturday	10		
11	**Total**	**160**		

Lining up the text in a cell

You can make the text in a spreadsheet line up on the left or right side, or arrange it centrally. You do this by highlighting the cells you want to change and then clicking on a button at the top of the screen. They are usually buttons such as:

左 left makes the text or number line up
on the left edge of the cell

左 centre makes the text or number centred
about the middle of the cell

左 right makes the text or number line up
on the right edge of the cell

In the example spreadsheet below, all of column B has been centred. To do something to a complete column, you just click on the letter heading at the top of the column, in this case the letter B.

	A	B	C	D
1	Weekly journeys by car			
2				
3	Day	Distance (miles)		
4	Sunday	5		
5	Monday	25		
6	Tuesday	43		
7	Wednesday	27		
8	Thursday	22		
9	Friday	28		
10	Saturday	10		
11	Total	160		

Using a spreadsheet to make calculations

The cost of travelling a mile is 5 pence. So if you multiply the distance travelled on each day by 5 you get the cost of travelling for that day, in pence. If you add up the costs for each day, you get the total weekly cost of travel. You can set up the example spreadsheet to make these calculations for you.

You can put a 5 into cells C4 to C10. (You can centre the column, as well as putting a bold heading in cell C3.)

	A	B	C	D
1	**Weekly journeys by car**			
2				
3	**Day**	**Distance (miles)**	**Cost per mile (p)**	
4	Sunday	5	5	
5	Monday	25	5	
6	Tuesday	43	5	
7	Wednesday	27	5	
8	Thursday	22	5	
9	Friday	28	5	
10	Saturday	10	5	
11	**Total**	**160**		

You can now put a formula into cell D4 to calculate the cost of travel for Sunday. This formula would be B4∗C4. The ∗ symbol is used as a multiplication sign.

To calculate the cost of travel on each of the other days, a similar formula must be put into each of the cells D5 to D10. To calculate the total cost of travel for the whole week, a sum is put in cell D11. The spreadsheet should end up like this. (Here the formula is shown in each cell, and not the result of the calculation.)

	A	B	C	D
1	**Weekly journeys by car**			
2				
3	**Day**	**Distance (miles)**	**Cost per mile (p)**	
4	Sunday	5	5	=B4∗C4
5	Monday	25	5	=B5∗C5
6	Tuesday	43	5	=B6∗C6
7	Wednesday	27	5	=B7∗C7
8	Thursday	22	5	=B8∗C8
9	Friday	28	5	=B9∗C9
10	Saturday	10	5	=B10∗C10
11	**Total**	**160**	**Total cost**	**=SUM (D4:D10)**

On screen, with the results of the calculations included, the spreadsheet will finally look like this.

	A	B	C	D
1	Weekly journeys by car			
2				
3	Day	Distance (miles)	Cost per mile (p)	
4	Sunday	5	5	25
5	Monday	25	5	125
6	Tuesday	43	5	215
7	Wednesday	27	5	135
8	Thursday	22	5	110
9	Friday	28	5	140
10	Saturday	10	5	50
11	Total	160	Total cost	800

If the number of miles were to change on Wednesday from 27 to 42 then you could type 42 into cell B7. The figure in D7 would automatically change to 210, and the total cost in cell D11 would change to 875.

Printing your spreadsheet

You can print your spreadsheet any time you like. There will be a button at the top of the screen with a picture of a printer on it. Click on this button. What appears on the paper should be exactly what you have created on the screen.

Making decisions

You can use spreadsheets to help you make decisions. For example, you might be planning to run a small company that buys and sells drinks. You buy them at one price and sell them at another. You want to make your profit as large as possible. One way of doing this is to sell the drinks at a high price. However, if your prices are too high people will not buy the drinks and you will be stuck with a lot of stock that you cannot sell. You could create the following spreadsheet to make your position clearer.

Cell E2 contains a formula: (C2–B2)*D2. This is replicated in cells E3 to E6. Cell F7 contains a formula: SUM(E2:E6). This gives the total profit.

With this spreadsheet on the screen, you can ask 'what if' questions to see the effects of different actions.

	A	B	C	D	E	F
1	Item	Purchase cost (p)	Selling price (p)	Number sold each day	Profit (p)	Total profit (p)
2	Orange Juice	18	24	12	72	
3	Cola	25	30	10	50	
4	Lemonade	14	20	15	90	
5	Blackcurrant Juice	20	25	4	20	
6	Milk	25	30	3	15	
7						247

Example 1

What if you increased the selling price of lemonade (the best seller) to 22 pence? What effect would this have on the profit?

	A	B	C	D	E	F
1	Item	Purchase cost (p)	Selling price (p)	Number sold each day	Profit (p)	Total profit (p)
2	Orange Juice	18	24	12	72	
3	Cola	25	30	10	50	
4	Lemonade	14	22	15	120	
5	Blackcurrant Juice	20	25	4	20	
6	Milk	25	30	3	15	
7						277

Example 2

What if the supplier increases the cost of cola from 25 pence to 29 pence? What effect will this have on the profit?

	A	B	C	D	E	F
1	Item	Purchase cost (p)	Selling price (p)	Number sold each day	Profit (p)	Total profit (p)
2	Orange Juice	18	24	12	72	
3	Cola	29	30	10	10	
4	Lemonade	14	22	15	120	
5	Blackcurrant Juice	20	25	4	20	
6	Milk	25	30	3	15	
7						237

This would have quite a bad effect on the profit so the selling price of cola might have to increase. You would have to decide on a selling price that would make a good profit and yet not put people off buying cola.

Exercise

The following spreadsheet shows the number of stuffed toys sold by a shop in a week. Answer the questions below. Each question is based on the original spreadsheet so you may have to reload it between questions.

	A	B	C	D	E
1	**Stuffed toys sold in a week**				
2	**Item**	**Purchase price (p)**	**Selling price (p)**	**Number sold**	**Profit (p)**
3	Parrot	400	700	3	=(C3–B3)*D3
4	Dog	600	900	5	=(C4–B4)*D4
5	Penguin	350	790	8	=(C5–B5)*D5
6	Hedgehog	1200	2000	2	=(C6–B6)*D6
7	Lion	640	1200	8	=(C7–B7)*D7
8	Bear	1580	2400	9	=(C8–B8)*D8
9	Cat	560	900	12	=(C9–B9)*D9
10	Owl	340	580	4	=(C10–B10)*D10
11					
12	Total profit (p)				=SUM(E3:E10)
13	**Total profit (£)**				**=E12/100**

1 What would be the total profit (£) if the number of lions sold were to increase to 12?

2 What would be the total profit (£) if the number of penguins sold fell to 3?

3 What would be the total profit (£) if the selling price of bears were to increase to £26.00?

4 What would be the total profit (£) if the purchase price of dogs increased to £8.00?

5 Which would give the bigger profit:
    a) increasing the selling price of owls to £7.00?
    b) increasing the selling price of parrots to £8.00?

Evaluation of a spreadsheet program

When you have been using a spreadsheet program for a while, you will have an idea of how useful it is in doing what you want it to do.

To evaluate a spreadsheet program, you should think about a number of things.

1 How much faster was it to use the spreadsheet instead of doing all the calculations by hand?
2 How good or bad was the spreadsheet in editing the cells?
3 How easy or hard was it to change the look of the cells to bold, italic and so on?
4 How easy or hard was it to change the size and font of the text?
5 How easy or hard was it to change the position of the text in the cell so that it was aligned on the left or right, or centred?
6 How easy or hard was it to change the content of a cell and see the other cells change?
7 How easy or hard was it to print what you wanted?

In an evaluation, do not talk about whether you enjoyed doing the project. Always make remarks about what you were doing, and *not* how you felt about it.

Control

What is control?

In computer terms, the word control means to make something work in the way you want. A computer can control many devices.

Drawing on screen

You can give the computer simple commands to move an object around a screen making a picture of, say, a house. These commands are usually written in a **programming language** called **Logo.** Logo has many instructions, but the main ones are to move forwards or backwards and to turn right (clockwise) or left (anticlockwise).

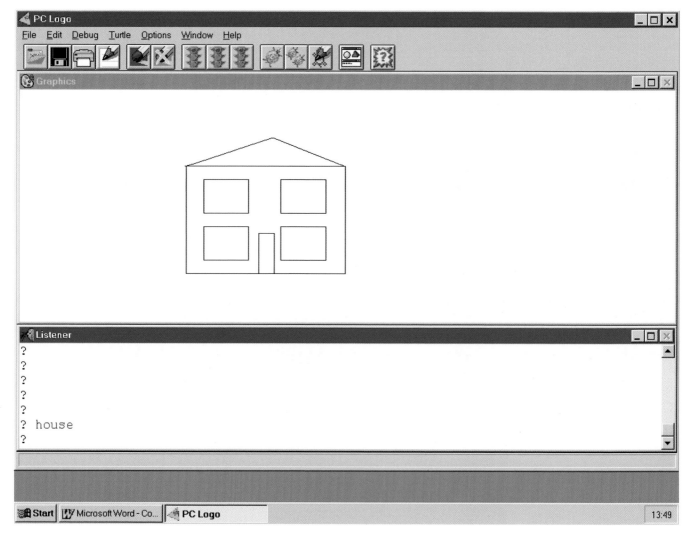

Using simple commands you can create all kinds of drawings on screen, such as this house.

Floor robots

As well as controlling an object on the screen, you can use a computer to control the movements of a real device called a floor turtle. A floor turtle is a simple robot that can turn either clockwise or anticlockwise and move either forwards or backwards. Using these simple movements, the turtle can go in any direction. Some floor turtles have a pen to trace the path on a large sheet of paper (see page 9).

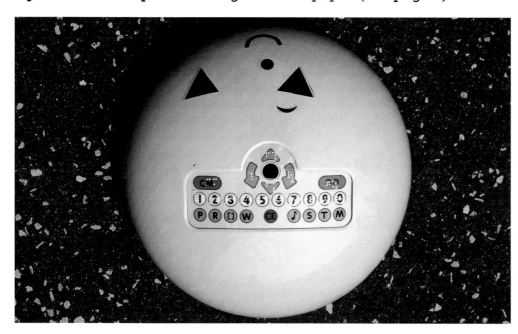

Some floor turtles do not have to be connected to the computer for them to work. Some have a special pad on top that can be used to make them move in any direction.

The computer can also be used to control a buggy. A buggy can be programmed to perform similar actions to a turtle, but it contains sensors that tell the computer when something has happened to the buggy. For example, a switch at the front could send data back to the computer to tell it when the buggy has hit a wall. You can build your own floor buggy from a kit, and connect it to your computer.

Other external devices

A computer can be used to control other real devices, such as heaters, lights, windows and machinery. Sensors tell the computer what is happening in the external environment, and the computer uses the instructions in its control program to turn the devices on and off as required.

If you want to control devices using a computer, you need to place an **interface unit** between the computer and what you are controlling. This is used to convert the data the computer sends out to a form that the devices can understand.

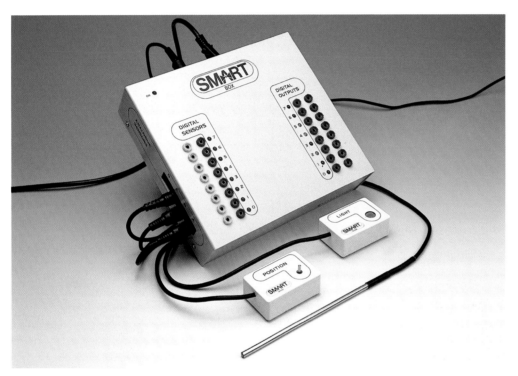

This interface unit allows a computer to control the internal environment in a greenhouse. It controls devices such as the windows, water sprinklers and heaters, to keep the greenhouse at the right temperature and humidity.

Controlling a screen image

The Logo programming language can be used to control a turtle on a screen. The language has many instructions. Some of them are shown in the table below.

Instruction	Meaning
FORWARD *n*	Move *n* cm forward
BACKWARD *n*	Move *n* cm backward
LEFT *t*	Turn left *t* degrees
RIGHT *t*	Turn right *t* degrees
PEN DOWN	Place the pen on the paper
PEN UP	Lift the pen off the paper

The distance to move from the turtle's current position is represented by a number n. The amount to turn from the way the turtle is currently pointing is represented by an angle t. (Different versions of Logo may use slightly different instructions.)

To draw a shape, the Logo program first needs to be loaded from the hard disk into the main memory of your computer. You normally do this by double clicking the left mouse button while you are pointing at the Logo icon on the screen.

You can control the turtle by typing in one of the instructions. The turtle moves after you have typed each instruction.

FORWARD 50   moves the turtle forward 50 units towards the north (Logo usually starts off by pointing the turtle towards the north)

LEFT 45   turns the turtle 45° anticlockwise

FORWARD 40   moves the turtle 40 units in the direction it is pointing

PEN UP   lifts the 'pen' off the screen – any further movements of the turtle do not leave a line

PEN DOWN   lowers the 'pen' so that lines are drawn on the screen again

Using these instructions, you can draw many shapes. You may have to clear the screen of any drawings before you start a new one. The instruction for this is usually CLEARSCREEN or CS.

Exercise

Here are some shapes you can try to draw using the instructions given above.
You will need to decide what values of n and t are needed to make these shapes.
You may want to look at Example 1 on the next page first.

Example 1 – square

To draw a square you can use the instructions:

PEN DOWN
FORWARD 50
LEFT 90
FORWARD 50
LEFT 90
FORWARD 50
LEFT 90
FORWARD 50
LEFT 90

Example 2 – loops

The square example above was very repetitive. If the same instructions are to be used many times you can put them in a **loop** and say how many times you want those instructions to be obeyed.

The instructions to be repeated are usually placed inside a set of square brackets. Before the brackets you type REPEAT followed by the number of times you want the instructions to be repeated. So to draw the square using a loop you would type:

REPEAT 4 [FORWARD 50 LEFT 90]

Example 3 – procedures

You can teach the computer a new instruction by creating a **procedure**. A procedure is the name given to a set of instructions for a particular action. For example, the procedure for drawing a square could be written as:

TO SQUARE
REPEAT 4 [FORWARD 50 LEFT 90]
END

The TO tells the computer you are about to create a procedure. SQUARE is the name you have given to the procedure. END is the way you tell the computer that you have finished writing the procedure.

Notice that when you type the procedure the turtle on the screen does not move. To get the computer to draw a square, you must type in the name of the procedure:

SQUARE

It will then draw a square at whatever position the turtle is on the screen.

Exercise

Create the procedure SQUARE as explained (see page 52).
Now create the following procedure:

TO ROTATE
REPEAT 20 [SQUARE LEFT 18]
END

See the picture that this procedure draws by typing:

CLEARSCREEN
ROTATE

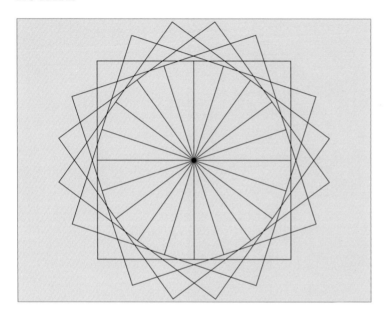

The diagram you get using the ROTATE procedure should look like this.

Example 4 – lifting the pen

In some cases, you may wish to lift the pen off the paper. One way of drawing a dashed line is using the following instructions:

RIGHT 90
PEN DOWN
FORWARD 50
PEN UP
FORWARD 50
PEN DOWN
FORWARD 50
PEN UP
FORWARD 50
PEN DOWN
FORWARD 50
PEN UP
FORWARD 50

This simple program should result in:

You could also use a REPEAT instruction to make this dashed line.

RIGHT 90
REPEAT 3 [PEN DOWN FORWARD 50 PEN UP FORWARD 50]

As you see, with some simple instructions it is possible to make very interesting shapes.

Exercise

Try making the following shapes on screen. In some cases, you will have to lift the pen off the paper.

Saving and loading your work

The way you save your work will depend on the particular version of Logo you are using. You might have to type SAVE to save your procedures, or you might have to 'drag and drop' your procedure into a directory. Your teacher will tell you how to save from your version of Logo.

To use a procedure you have already saved, you will have to load it into Logo. Again, the way you do this will depend on the version of Logo you are using. You might have to type LOAD <procedure name>, or double click on the procedure icon. Your teacher will tell you how to load into your version of Logo.

Controlling an external device

To see how a computer can be used to control devices, you could build a model. For example, you could construct a simple model greenhouse from a kit, and use a computer to control devices that will maintain the right temperature for growing plants. To control the devices, you need to use an interface unit (see page 50) and a set of instructions, or program in the computer.

This is a model greenhouse constructed from a kit, which can be controlled using a computer.

This simple program could be used to control the temperature in the greenhouse:

```
REPEAT FOREVER
[
IF temperature IS ABOVE 30 THEN [ open_windows switch_off_heater ]
IF temperature IS BELOW 10 THEN [ close_windows switch_on_heater ]
]
```

- ■ temperature   a value in degrees Celsius taken from a temperature sensor inside the greenhouse
- ■ open_windows   the name of a procedure that opens the windows
- ■ switch_on_heater   the name of a procedure that switches on a heater
- ■ close_windows   the name of a procedure that closes the windows
- ■ switch_off_heater   the name of a procedure that switches off a heater

Commands like switch_off_heater have lines that separate the words. Commands cannot include spaces, so these lines keep the words together as a single readable command. It is clearer to do this than to type switchoffheater, for example.

Devices that respond to signals

Remote control

Many everyday devices respond to signals from remote control handsets.

Televisions, VCRs and satellite decoders all respond to signals from remote control handsets to change the channels or settings.

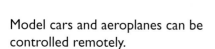

Model cars and aeroplanes can be controlled remotely.

Cars can be locked and unlocked remotely.

Traffic lights

Traffic lights are controlled to produce lights in a set pattern: red, red and orange together, green, orange, red. The control system can be set up to try to ensure that traffic flows smoothly.

In some cases, the control system is set up so that the lights on one road at a junction are red for longer because there is more traffic on the other road.

Computers can control the flow of traffic at a junction by controlling the way the traffic lights change.

In other cases, the lights are always red until traffic approaches. There is a sensor on the road to signal when traffic is coming.

Lights at different junctions can be co-ordinated to work together. For example, the control system could be set up so that when one set of lights turns green to let the cars through, the lights at the next junction up the road will also turn green as the cars approach.

Evaluation of a control package

When you have used either Logo or a control program for a while, you will have an idea of how useful it is in doing what you want it to do.

To evaluate a program, you should think about a number of things.

For Logo

1 How easy or hard was it to move the turtle?
2 How easy or hard was it to draw a shape?
3 Were the instructions easy to remember?
4 How easy or hard was it to load and save the turtle procedures?
5 How easy or hard was it to print the instructions?
6 How easy or hard was it to print the diagrams?
7 How easy or hard was it to change the shape of the turtle?

For a control program

1 How easy or hard was it to give instructions to control a system like a model greenhouse?
2 How easy or hard was it to save and load your instructions?
3 How easy or hard was it to print your instructions?
4 Was there something you wanted to do that the program would not let you do?

In an evaluation, do not talk about whether you enjoyed doing the project. Always make remarks about what you were doing, and *not* how you felt about it.

Glossary

application   A program designed to carry out a task, such as a word processor or a spreadsheet.

backspace   The 'delete the last character typed' key on the keyboard. Usually a long key at the top right of the main letters.

caret   A flashing straight line on the screen that shows you where the letters will go when you press a key on the keyboard (also called the cursor or arrow).

CD-ROM   A portable disk on which nothing can be recorded. It usually has a capacity of 600 MB. Unlike the data on both floppy and hard disks, which is stored magnetically, the data stored on a CD-ROM is read using a laser beam.

cells   A spreadsheet is divided into boxes known as cells. The columns are referred to by letters, and the rows by numbers. A particular cell is identified by a letter and a number. The letter usually comes first, e.g. cell B5.

clip art   Pictures and diagrams that have been created by someone else. They often come on a CD-ROM containing around 3000 pictures.

computer   A device that is used to take in data and store it. The user of the computer will often do something with the data retrieved from the computer.

computer aided design (CAD)   An application that enables you to draw designs on the screen. These designs can be very accurate engineering drawings for industry or simple sketches to see what a design might look like. The computer can produce a three-dimensional image of a design to give an idea of what the final object could really look like.

computer program   A set of instructions that the computer can understand. A word processor is an example of a program. Programs are loaded into the computer's main memory from storage devices. Once in the main memory of the computer they operate at very fast speeds.

concept keyboard   A large flat surface that is divided into squares (also called an overlay keyboard). When one of the squares is pressed an action occurs on the screen. A computer program controls what happens when you press the concept keyboard.

control   In computer terms, this means to make machines work in the way you want. A computer can control many devices such as a floor turtle or a buggy.

cursor   A flashing straight line on the screen that shows you where the letters will go when you press a key on the keyboard (also called the caret or arrow).

data handling program   A program that allows you to search, edit and make additions to a database.

database   A structured collection of data all of which have some connection. For example, the complete set of records about all the students in a school is known as a database.

desktop publishing (DTP)   A computer program that allows you to position text and pictures on the screen. Pictures and text are usually kept in frames on the screen that can be moved to any position you like. Newspapers are created using DTP packages.

digital camera   This is used to transfer pictures to a computer. It is operated by pressing a button to take a picture. The picture is then stored in the camera.

directory   A place for storing documents or other data files together so that you can find them again easily.

document   A piece of saved work from a word processor.

dot-matrix printer   Printer that produces an image on the paper by firing metal pins at an inked ribbon. They are quite noisy machines and relatively slow but they are very cheap to buy.

enter   A large key to the right of the letter keys on a keyboard, which is used to force the caret (or cursor) on to a new line.

field   Each record in a database is split up into a number of sections, e.g. a person's name, sex, address and so on. Each of these sections is known as a field.

find   To find information from a database you must be able to search it. This is called a query or a find in some data handling programs.

floor robot   A device on wheels, such as a turtle or a buggy, which can be controlled by a computer. It can turn either clockwise or anticlockwise and move either forwards or backwards. It sometimes has a pen that can be used to trace its path on a large sheet of paper.

floppy disk   This can be used to store data or programs. The disk, and hence the data on the disk, can be passed from one computer to another. Floppy disks are usually used to store programs, text, small pictures and short sounds.

font   The shape of the letters is called the font.

formula   A calculation to be carried out using numbers from other cells in a spreadsheet. To tell the spreadsheet that you are going to enter a formula, you must start typing with an equals (=) sign, e.g. =A2+B2.

frame   In DTP programs and word processing programs, pictures and text are usually kept in frames on the screen that can be moved to any position you like.

gigabyte   A unit for measuring how much data can be stored on a disk. One gigabyte is 1024 megabytes (or about 1000 megabytes).

graphics   Any kind of drawing, chart or picture that you have created or has come from a clip art disk.

hard copy   Printed copy of what you see on screen, produced using a printer or a plotter.

hard disk   A high capacity disk that is fitted to the inside of the main processor box of a computer. It is not normally removable. The size of the hard disk is measured in megabytes or gigabytes. It is constantly revolving and so stores and retrieves data very quickly. A hard disk can store programs, text, pictures, animation, movies and sound.

hardware   The parts of the computer that you can see and touch.

highlight   If you want to do something to a part of your text you must highlight it first. The area highlighted will change to white writing on black instead of black writing on white. You can then do something to the text, such as make it bold.

information technology (IT)   Using computers to store and sort out information is called information technology.

ink-jet printer   Printer that produces an image by spraying ink on the paper. Ink-jet printers are quiet, fast, and can produce high quality images. However, they are expensive to run because the ink cartridges are costly to replace.

interface unit   A piece of hardware placed between the computer and a device that the computer is to control. It is used to convert the data the computer sends out to a form the device can understand.

Internet   A collection of computers around the world from which you can obtain data by searching in a similar way as you would search a database.

justification   Arrangement of a piece of text so that the left and right edges are straight.

kilobyte   A unit for measuring how much data can be stored on a disk. One kilobyte is 1024 bytes (or about 1000 bytes).

laser printer   Printer that operates in a similar way to a photocopier. Laser printers are very quiet, very fast and can produce a very high quality printout, but are expensive to buy and run.

Logo   A computer programming language used to give simple commands to move an object around a screen. Logo has many instructions, but the main ones are to move forwards or backwards or to turn right (clockwise) or left (anticlockwise).

loop   When writing a program in a computer programming language such as Logo, if the same instructions are to be repeated many times you can put them in a loop and say how many times you want them to be obeyed.

main memory   Programs are loaded into the computer's main memory, or random access memory (RAM), from storage devices. Once in the main memory of the computer, programs operate at very fast speeds.

megabyte   A unit for measuring how much data can be stored on a disk. One megabyte is 1024 kilobytes (or about one million bytes).

menu   A list of choices on the screen that can be selected from, by clicking the left mouse button.

model   To use a computer to represent a real life situation. A model is a description of how something works. Often computer models use mathematics to describe how a situation works.

monitor   An output device resembling a television screen. The screen shows you what is being done on the computer.

mouse   A hand-held device that you slide over a flat surface, to control the pointer on the computer screen. It has one or more buttons on top – clicking the button makes some action happen, e.g. choosing something from a menu.

numeric data   Numbers that are stored in, say, spreadsheet cells or database fields.

open   This term means that you want to load a document or other file of data from the disk, to change or edit it.

package   A program designed to carry out a task, such as a word processor or a spreadsheet.

peripherals   Extra devices that can be attached to a computer, such as a printer or a scanner.

printer   An output device that produces a record of your work on paper (a hard copy).

procedure   A set of instructions in the Logo programming language.

programming language   The words used to write instructions that the computer will obey make up a programming language such as Logo.

query   The question you create to search a database.

record   A set of related data, such as data about one student in a school database.

relationship   In a database, the connection between the field being searched and the value you are looking for is called the relationship, e.g. 'identical to' or 'less than'.

save   Store data on a disk so that it can be retrieved later.

scanner   This is used to transfer pictures to a computer. Once the pictures are in the computer you can alter them or add them to other documents. Motorised flat-bed scanners are quite accurate. Scanners can be either black and white or colour.

screen   An output device resembling a television screen, which shows you what is being done on the computer.

search   The act of finding all the records in a database that match a given value, e.g. all students named Smith.

software   The programs that control the computer.

sound card   A piece of electronics added to a computer to give it the ability to produce good quality sound.

spreadsheet   A grid of boxes or cells each of which can contain text, a number or a formula.

string data   Data that is not numeric, which is stored in, say, spreadsheet cells or database fields. String data is also called text data, and includes letters or words.

text   A collection of letters, usually in the form of words.

value   The object that you are searching for in a database field, e.g. Smith.

visual display unit (VDU)   An output device resembling a television screen, which shows you what is being done on the computer.

word processor   A computer program that allows you to enter text, alter it and save it. You can also print your work. You can make the words bigger, change the style of the letters, line up the edges of the writing, and so on. You can make the text **bold,** underlined or in *italics*. Many word processors can also import pictures such as clip art or even graphics that you have created yourself.

Index

application 3
arithmetic symbols 39

backspace 15

calculations with a spreadsheet
   42–44
caret 15
CD-ROM 3, 6
cells 37
central processing unit 2
clip art 14
complex search 30
computer 2
computer aided design (CAD)
   14, 21–22
computer program 3
concept keyboard 11–12
control 48, 50–51, 55
cursor 15

data handling program 24, 26
databases 24–25, 34–35
decisions 44
desktop publishing 14, 20
digital cameras 12-13
directory 15
disk drive 2
document 15
dot-matrix printer 7
drawing 48

encyclopaedias 34
entering text 14
evaluation 23, 36, 47, 58

field 24
find 27
floor turtle 9, 49
floppy disk 4, 5
font 17
formula 38
frame 20

gigabyte 3
graphics 14
graphics tablet 12

handling data 24
hard copy 7
hard disk 5
hardware 3
highlighting 16, 40

Information Technology 2
ink-jet printer 8
interface unit 50
Internet 14, 35

joystick 11
justification 16

keyboard 2,10
kilobyte 3

laser printer 8
loading 14, 15, 27, 37, 40, 54
Logo 48

main memory 3
making decisions 44
megabyte 3
menu 10, 15, 18, 40
model 37
monitor 2, 7
mouse 10

numeric data 25, 26, 38

opening files 15
overlay keyboards 11–12

package 3
pen 53
peripherals 3
plotter 9
printers 3, 7–8

printing 19, 34, 44
procedure 52
programming language 48

query 27

random access memory (RAM)
   4
record 24
relationship 27
remote control 56–57
repeat 52
robots 9, 49

saving 15, 31, 40, 54
scanners 12–13
screen 2, 7
searching 27, 30
software 3
sorting 31
sound card 9
speakers 9
spreadsheet 37
storage 3–6
string data 25

television 56
text 14, 38
traffic lights 57
turtle 9, 49

value 27
VCR 56
visual display unit (VDU) 7

word processor 14

zip disk 6